SINGBIRD LESSONS
Presents

How to Go from Bad Singer to Good Singer

By: Elizabeth Ann Wallace

Copyright © 2017 by Elizabeth Ann Wallace and Published by Brian Ernest Hayward for Hayward House Publishing
Published by Hayward House and Big Book Box A Member of the Brian Hayward Group

All rights reserved. No part of this publication may be reproduced, stored in a retrieval system, or transmitted, in any form or by any means, electronic, mechanical, photocopying, recording, or otherwise, without the prior written permission of the publis her. For information and inquiries , address Hayward House publishing and Hayward Press, 4613 Lanier drive, 4th Floor, Savannah, Ga 31405, or call (912) 224- 7502.

Library of Congress Cataloging-in-Publication Data
Hayward, Brian. TITLE=**Singbird Lessons**, Journaling for success in your life / Brian Hayward. p. cm.

ISBN-13:
978-1981532025

ISBN-10:
1981532021

Self-control. 2. Self-management (Psychology) 3. Success. 4. Success in business. Big Book Box Press books are available at special discounts for bulk purchases in the U.S. by corporat io ns, institut io ns, and other organizat io ns . For more information, please contact the Special Markets Department at the Big Book Box Books Group, 4613 Lanier drive, 4th Floor, Savannah, Ga 31405,or call (912) 224- 7502, or visit us at:

https://www.amazon.com/Brian-Ernest-Hayward/e/B06XT464NM

AUTHOR/SONGSTRESS BIOGRAPHY

Elizabeth Wallace is a passionate Author and Inspirational Singer and Speaker for the Lord Jesus Christ, internationally known for her unwavering dedication to encouraging positive change through the power of words. From religious and success books, to Christian Audio CD's Her Clear and Concise Christian writings touch on over 50 different subjects.

Today, all of Elizabeth's publications are sold worldwide across multiple formats (Paperback, Kindle, Large Print, itunes, Apple Music, Tidal, Spotify, and all media outlets) and are translated into 21 different languages. She has also participated in over 20 speaking engagements spanning over 13 states.

PUBLISHER BIOGRAPHY

Hayward Publishing Company led by Brian Ernest Hayward is a6 Global Leader in Christian Literature. **Owner Brian Hayward,** is a passionate Author and Inspirational Speaker, internationally known for his unwavering dedication to creating positive change through the power of words. From religious and success books, to adult coloring books and artist how-tos, his writings touch on over 400 different subjects.

Today, all of Brian's publications are sold worldwide across multiple formats (Paperback, Kindle, and Large Print) and are translated into 21 different languages. He has also participated in over 100 speaking engagements spanning over 38 states.

INTRODUCTION

 *I* *was taught by my teacher, Pastor Bill Winston, this prayer. This prayer has served me well, and in due time it will serve you well. Father I come before you in Jesus name, thank you for the anointing that's on me and these lips of clay. I know that because of your blessing, I speak this word today with excellency, accuracy, and boldness.*

I thank you for thinking through my mind and speaking through my lips and this word will come forth unhindered, and unchecked by any outside force. Now I give you the praise for it and I fully expect signs, wonders, and miracles to confirm your word preached in Jesus name, Amen! This is a book about the "new creation" God has made me through Christ Jesus. Be inspired as you read toward greatness and achievement.

YOUR PORTION

Another of My teachers is Pastor Dr. Uebert Angel. Dr Uebert Angel is a very good bible teacher. Check out his books very soon, if you have not already. He mentioned this verse in his book entitled: God's Get Rich Quick Scheme. He notes, "Thus saith the LORD, thy Redeemer, the Holy One of Israel; I am the LORD thy God which teacheth thee to profit, which leadeth thee by the way that thou shouldest go. Isaiah 48:17 Do you see that, he teaches you to profit, by his word, by his spiritual laws, he wants to lead you the way you should go and that way is not into a financial wilderness, it's to take you to a place of the overflow for Jesus came so that you should have life and have it abundantly.

Lack is not your portion, sickness is not your portion, poverty is not your portion, and generational curses are not your portion. Work towards a seed, find good ground, sow your seed and act upon what you have sowed for, you will surely come back with a testimony.

MAKE THIS CONFESSION BEFORE READING THIS BOOK

MAKE THIS FULL CONFESSION EACH NIGHT FOR THE NEXT 30 DAYS. "I am a winner. I am blessed coming by in and blessed going out. I am blessed in all my efforts. I am blessed in all my undertakings. I am blessed even when I merely try. God's grace gives me greater victories even when I start later than others. Everything I put my hands to is blessed. Everything I show interest in acquiring, I am blessed with achieving. My mind is blessed in everything I think of. My ideas are blessed. My ideas are blessed with heavenly creativity. God prepared my deliverance before the foundation of the earth and he has already made all crooked places straight and opened doors that men have said are impossible to open. I am blessed with God's word

I keep sound wisdom and discretion. Wisdom resides in my heart and knowledge is pleasant to my soul. Discretion preserves me. Understanding keeps me and delivers me from all evil. My ways are ways of pleasantness and all my paths are peace. Thank You, Father, I always find wisdom for she says, "I love them that love me; And those that seek me early shall find me." I trust in the Lord with all my heart, and lean not to my own understanding.

I am born of incorruptible seed; And I walk and live by faith. Wisdom leads me when I go; keeps me when I sleep, and speaks with me when I wake. I refuse to accept any lies from the devil. The Holy Spirit is my Teacher, and guides me into all truth.

Table of Contents

Psalm 101:1

I will sing of lovingkindness and justice, To You, O LORD, I will sing praises.

By: Elizabeth Ann Wallace

<u>About the Structure of This Book</u>

- **PART 1: HOW TO GO FROM BAD SINGER TO GOOD SINGER**

- **PART 2: SINGING COURSES**

- **PART 3: VOICE LESSONS**

Part 1:
How to go from Bad Singer to Good Singer?

Chapter 1

Benefits of Singing Lessons

Psalm 33:1-3

"Sing for joy in the LORD, O you righteous ones; Praise is becoming to the upright. Give thanks to the LORD with the lyre; Sing praises to Him with a harp of ten strings. Sing to Him a new song; Play skillfully with a shout of joy."

Psalm 96:1-2

"Sing to the LORD a new song; Sing to the LORD, all the earth. Sing to the LORD, bless His name; Proclaim good tidings of His salvation from day to day."

There are many benefits of taking singing classes, and they not only incorporate the vocal chords but in addition your regular life too. Singing lessons could be taken to boost your present vocals or to find out a brand-new genre of songs, whatever the motive, never forget to pick the best singing lesson alternative which suits you the most. By deciding on the best choice, you stand to reap the most benefits from it. Listed below are a couple of benefits of picking the most suitable choice for your singing courses.

• Learning by a reputable voice coach can't just enhance your singing ability but can also cause you to a much better public speaker since you learn on the best way best to control and regulate your voice and the way to create inflections in it also.

• It will help build confidence in yourself and the fear of standing before a person and acting reduces greatly. Additionally, it educates you on how best to fortify your lungs so that your voice could be strong enough to be noticed hundreds of feet off.

• You know quite thoroughly concerning the vocal anatomy and so once you use it you can envision the way that your voice flows through from inside. This enhances your creativity and can assist in figuring out where you went wrong on a specific note and why, this then assists in boosting your voice too.

• The classes include breathing methods and rigorous discipline that only helps in vocal instruction and maintenance but may also be utilized as a stepping stone to present a general exercise regimen on your daily life together with the discipline and decision it takes.

Additionally, it aids in reducing overall anxiety and relaxing your entire body in a sense much like meditation.

• Singing lessons also instruct you on how to tune properly, a lot of individuals simply hear rather than hear, many pupils are tone deaf and cannot pinpoint precisely that notice is going wrong, therefore singing courses not only assist you to utilize your chords nicely but also teach you about how to tune properly.

• Additionally, they can enhance overall endurance and vitality levels.

• It gets the imagination flowing and enables you blend and match your regular thereby making you a much better singer.

• Singing may be a type of treatment since you're able to sing about your deepest feelings and be mentally alleviated.

Chapter 2

The way to be a singer is something a lot people want

"*Psalm 5:11*

But let all who take refuge in You be glad, Let them ever sing for joy; And may You shelter them, That those who love Your name may exult in You.

Psalm 9:11

Sing praises to the LORD, who dwells in Zion; Declare among the peoples His deeds.

"

The way to be a singer is something a lot people want, but just a few can reach this dream. Many men and women think that singing is much easier said than done but that is not correct. It isn't important if you simply have a modicum of singing abilities, you can experience achievement if you've got the fire and the driveway. Below are a few pointers that will help you to be a great singer.

Get Yourself Ready

Getting yourself prepared regarding your singing abilities is your very first step into becoming a singer. The simple fact that you're a gifted singer does not mean that you should not attend a couple of professional voice training sessions. Adopt a fantastic eating habit and do not consume food which will adversely impact your vocal cord like too hot or too cold drinks especially before singing.

Select Your Song

It is critical that you identify your vocal selection, because voice types are acceptable for singing kinds of tune and thus it is mandatory that you determine the song kind that will blend nicely with your voice. Is your voice intended for slow or rapid tunes? It is possible to try singing other kinds of songs, but do this once you've gained the control over the one which perfectly matches you.

Find Out More Songs

Additionally, investing in singing courses can allow you to be a singer. This will let you make music instead of simply singing together it. Do not be surprised if you get started writing songs. Occasionally, it is not all about having a wonderful voice; the tune is the thing that attracts people's attention.

Observing

1 way about the best way best to be a singer would be to observe the ideal. Take out time to see plenty of performances of your favorite singers and actors; be aware of the singing performances and styles. Observe their abilities and goal to develop your own distinctive style out of theirs.

Recordings

Be certain that you record your music on a CD. Your next move is to ship your "presentation" to record labels. Send to as many tags as you can to get attention from many them. Be certain that the songs you listed are of top quality, or else it will not be considered. The web is also a wonderful place to promote your singing career. As an example, you can construct a site where all your songs presentations are all uploaded. Make it a point to socialize with another artist to be able to make an avenue that you learn from these.

Chapter 3

Even though a great deal of folks

Angels Singing
Job 38:7
When the morning stars sang together And all the sons of God shouted for joy?

Those Singing Praise
Ezra 3:11
They sang, praising and giving thanks to the LORD, saying, "For He is good, for His lovingkindness is upon Israel forever." And all the people shouted with a great shout when they praised the LORD because the foundation of the house of the LORD was laid.

Even though a great deal of folks is into singing, make it at the karaoke bar, in front or an audience, or even at the shower, not everybody understands how to sing correctly. To become as great as Whitney Houston, or some other high-caliber listeners, it demands absolute talent, commitment, and suitable singing courses. Even when you're born with a fantastic voice, you must take singing courses that will assist you with the ideal method in singing correctly.

Becoming a fantastic singer isn't accomplished by taking shortcuts, as a lot of men and women think. For gift such as singing, a solid foundation is essential. This is the reason why it's best to enroll your children in singing courses while they're young, and they have more space for advancement. This can be important if your kid is into singing and fantasies of being a professional singer at the future. As a parent, it will not be hard to discover a music college, because singing lessons for kids are extremely popular nowadays.

To learn how to sing, enrolling at a voice training college may be a significant help. It is possible to use the world wide web to look for a great college that might only be near your property. It is possible to use the quick links in sites to locate a college that fits your need for a voice student. Many educators that provide singing courses are either professional singers or trying performers who wish to make additional income. Find your perfect teacher by surfing music colleges across the net. They must be really devoted to take care of a variety of kinds of pupils, particularly children and people who didn't have background in singing.

 Enrolling your children that are great in singing but don't have the enthusiasm for music might not properly absorb the courses taken. So, to avoid wasting your money, be certain that the pupil you register to a singing school is enthusiastic enough. If you're the person who goal of taking courses, you also will need to estimate your reasons why you would like to achieve that. Would you need to be a professional singer? Or you only need to boost your gift?

Your mentor shouldn't only be great in singing, they should also have great connection. It wouldn't be inspiring whatsoever to visit a course with an extremely stiff teacher. The main thing in registering for a singing course is that you like your classes, and your decision to be a better singer develops increasingly.

Part 2:
Singing Courses

Chapter 4

Singing Courses: Are You Singing in A Single Straight Line?

Psalm 30:4
Sing praise to the LORD, you His godly ones, And give thanks to His holy name.

Psalm 47:6
Sing praises to God, sing praises; Sing praises to our King, sing praises.

Singing in a single straight line is quite typical of this untrained voice. To seem interesting once you sing, you're going to want to have the ability to operate your voice about as numerous highs and lows within a notice or a set of notes. Did that sound somewhat like Chinese? I will clarify.

Believe it or not, the clear majority of them are going to jump into a top octave, thereby restricting their range and linking notes quite awkwardly. It does not need to be like that. This is a issue even you're able to mend when you understand how and notably, once you're conscious of what is holding you back and inducing your restricted selection. This guide provides ideas about how to quickly expand your singing array in an easy-to-remember formula.

Decide on a word such as Malaika in the tune Malaika, for instance. And try talking the term. Are you currently really looking ordinary as you would when you speak to somebody? Do this exercise again, playing and recording back till you have got it correctly.

Going back to this stage in this article: Are you currently singing in a single straight line? Well, in case you do not use your complete range from language level up, you're restricting your scope. Therefore, singing in a single straight line is unavoidable since you essentially don't have any space to move. So, the next time that your vocal selection is maxing out prematurely, have a peek at where you are singing out of. If you are too high in the bottom end of the scale, then take it down a couple of octaves to where it is comfortable for you (because you want in address) and then work your way upwards.

It truly is that easy!
It's true, you are likely to need to train your voice with all the scales to be able to train your voice and your ear, but overall pay special attention to browsing the lower notes because it is the issue area which needs addressing in the event you fall from the class of the (shooting off to large notes onto a very low key). Trust me, it requires some time to break out from this awful habit, but if you would like to have a better vocal once you sing; to maintain greater hands; and, to broaden your scope, you'll need to make a concerted effort to learn how to sing along with your speaking voice, first.

Chapter 5

Splitting Away from Bad Habits.

Psalm 68:4

Sing to God, sing praises to His name; Lift up a song for Him who rides through the deserts,
Whose name is the LORD, and exult before Him.

Believe it or not, the toughest thing to do would be to split away from bad habits. Just those who succeed in doing so will become much better listeners. I have had calls from musicians (voice educated by me) whining their vocal performance on point had gone downhill and that they wish to come back for more courses. While I dig deep, it immediately becomes evident that they have gone back to their old ways; I visit my OWN pupil competing in a reality TV singing contest and performing NOTHING I instructed them to perform. It is like they never went to get vocal training in any way. The entire shebang: poor tossing, yelling and crying their way round a tune--I mean the entire flaming caboodle LIVE on TV. Incredible! I have seen my own pupils fall apart from the recording studio. Everything they have learned goes unexpectedly the window out. They even forget to BREATHE prior to a note. This book will consider the perils of regressing to your previous singing habits and the way to break the cycle in order to not only adopt and adapt to a different method, but also--and most importantly--to combine and blossom along with your new ability to be able to develop as a singer.

I can go on about this all day, these awful old singing customs are so endemic out there-seemingly they simply won't go off. All these issues can be fixed.   What then are the most frequent singing stumbling blocks and exactly what will be the proven tactics to steer clear of these.

NOT breathing in front of a notice is likely--in my estimation, and judging from students I've observed through time, among the most persistent issues. The way to repair this? Decide on a very simple verse in the song you prefer.

Search for 2 breathing areas--one in the start of a notice, and one at the center. Let us say your lineup looks like this: "The shadow of your smile [breathe] if you're gone"... Your breath ingestion being involving the words Smile and If. Your job is to exercise singing only that 1 point repeatedly whilst breathing in with the fall of the jaw in the very spot in precisely the exact same manner every time--where and whenever you feel like practicing.

NOT opening your mouth enough... that I occasionally refer to as singing with your mouth closed, is just another problem that will work its way back into your life for a contributor to trigger all the issues that go with this. Sing a tune you want, but look in the mirror to make sure that you're opening your mouth because possible. Practice in front of a mirror to get this one. It is the only real way to break the cycle.

NOT projecting your voice since you need to is another menace a singer ought to be especially tired of. It is so dead simple to seem dull again. Together with your voice that is fuller, state VAAAAGH and look in the mirror to realize your mouth fall to its entire extent as you're at it. And listen attentively to the way that your voice jobs better. When you've obtained your projection technique reigned back in, go right to your tune and use the exact same well-projected voice when you sing. So, another time awful old singing customs encroach upon your own vocal area, you will understand what to try to break loose!

Chapter 6

FANTASTIC SINGERS HAVE STRONG VOICES BUT!

Isaiah 44:23
Shout for joy, O heavens, for the LORD has done it! Shout joyfully, you lower parts of the earth; Break forth into a shout of joy, you mountains, O forest, and every tree in it; For the LORD has redeemed Jacob And in Israel He shows forth His glory.

Fantastic singers have strong voices but many them are unable to keep and preserve its quality over a time. There are a number of those who develop serious ailments that influence their throats and vocal cords. Some listeners harm their vocal cords due to an excessive amount of strain put on it and sometimes they shed the sound of the singing voice too. But they could stop these things from occurring if they understand how to keep up the high quality and the energy of the voices.

Singers will need to continue to keep their own bodies always in great health. Should they do so, they are not as prone to infections particularly the ones that may impact the pieces of their bodies that they utilize for singing. Staying healthy would include things like eating the ideal type of foods, doing routine exercises and having adequate time to rest and sleep. Besides these there are a few things that they must recall. They need to see that alcoholic in addition to carbonated beverages can cause some aggravation on the linings located from the neck region. They also must take notice that spicy foods can cause a while to go all the way up into the throat.

Regular men and women are advised to drink loads of water per day. The exact same goes with listeners but people who'd like to conserve their strong singing voice for a very long time must drink hot water as far as you can. They also ought to clinic self-discipline and prevent smoking such as second-hand smoking so to allow them to reduce their risks of developing certain sorts of cancer ailments. They must decide to live healthier lives if they wish to succeed and remain long in the audio market.

Singers must inspect labels of goods which they use. There are a few substances found in mouthwash which can result in injury to their vocal cords and other elements of their address organ such as. They'll also have to add appropriate breathing as well even while they're speaking so that they can lower the strain that's set on their own throats. If they find themselves in places where the weather is dry, they're also able to indulge in steam inhalations or else they are also able to assess whether a humidifier can be found.

Fantastic listeners may love having their strong voices till they grow old, but they must work on preserving their health and their complete well-being. They must comprehend how some kinds of foods and actions may favorably or negatively influence their health generally and their strong voice specifically.

Part 3:
Voice Lessons

Chapter 7

Singing Voice Lessons

Isaiah 49:13
Shout for joy, O heavens! And rejoice, O earth! Break forth into joyful shouting, O mountains!
For the LORD has comforted His people And will have compassion on His afflicted.

You must have heard Frank Sinatra stating, "there is not any business-like show business" nicely with all the money, glory and fame which accompanies a successful singing career he was incorrect. A number of these folks are natural listeners while some will willingly take singing voice classes and work hard to hone their own abilities.

Most of these organic singers frequently question the significance of shooting singing voice classes. In fact, whether you're a newcomer or a singer with a rather good control over the ability you always have the option to utilize singing voice classes to further boost your voice along with your comprehension. Singing voice classes are especially significant if singing is much more than only a hobby as as a professional you'll have to be aware of the finer points of this artwork. And singing voice classes will Allow You to gain an edge on another untrained voice.

The issue with self-educated singers is that they follow the 'view and learn technique'. That's they know by emulating a favorite performer. If you're among these, it is just natural that you pick up your favorite artist's style of singing, and customs good or poor. However, as a budding singer you won't ever can tell the right from the incorrect and you'll necessarily and kindly follow within this singer's foot measures. This is the area where singing voice classes will be convenient. In these lessons you'll be educated to do things the perfect way, unlearn a good deal of previous habits which might in fact be marring your own performance.

Additionally, each singer has their own blend of singing and voice attributes that can't be developed by simply imitating your favorite artists. Singing voice lessons can allow you to recognize your weaknesses and strengths. So that you're able to use your strengths to your very best advantage and focus on your weaknesses and create a style which suits you the very best.

However, it isn't quite as simple as it sounds. There are a plethora of voice coaches and colleges each claiming to be the ideal. So, finding the ideal school or trainer for singing voice courses might be a real job. Though every trainer will possess his/her identifying technique, all styles have their own demerits and values, using only 1 method to learn will rarely help you. A fantastic mentor will understand and identify your problems based on your own performance and produce a well-balanced approach that encompasses many unique practices.

In the end of the afternoon it's crucial to discover a mentor who knows that it is not the method but the result that matters the most. Thus, once you're looking out for a college be certain that you speak to a few trainers; attempt to obtain their perspectives on the various tactics and attempt to get information in their other pupils.

Finally, if you're hoping miracle remedies during singing voice courses you'll be sorely disappointed. These classes are by no means a fast fix or a magic potion to visit another octave or to create the voice assortment of an accomplished singer. They require patience, diligence and endurance to yield outcomes and you need to be prepared to spend the work, hard work and time required to get the goals that you would like.
An excellent artist gets greater by recognizing his limits and then accepting that he needs help to overcome these limitations and reach another level.

Chapter 7

ON A HIGH NOTE

Isaiah 52:9
Break forth, shout joyfully together, You waste places of Jerusalem; For the LORD has comforted His people, He has redeemed Jerusalem.

High notes are a few of the most essential facets of singing, since you cannot possess a huge performance without going higher inside your scope. Singers who sing in their own lower range are deemed excellent singers, but people who will sing those high notes are commended greatly. Thus, I cannot blame you for needing to learn how to sing high notes.

Singing high notes are not always something singers are born with, but really developed. There could be a few that have a natural talent at singing good, but there is a fantastic probability that they staged a lot to get up there and really make it sound great. If you would like to experience being up there in your scope, you ought to try yawning, maintaining that back throat opened. You do not wish to push it down, but marginally keep it started. You will realize that your voice feels much more relaxed. Before you ever strike a high note, you really must do this to prevent straining and potential tension.

The Apple Ah is really a wonderful method for singing high notes with clarity and improved tone. When you are stirring, open your mouth and act as if you're attempting to bite an apple. Sing a couple notes on your mid rage and then make it up as you become better. This also helps that yawning feeling to begin happening, so it is powerful.

• Breath support

Breathing is an important consideration to consider, as you cannot sing higher or low notes if you do not have sufficient breath support to carry up your voice there. Do this a few times to receive that airflow coming and to keep your breath powerful. What many singers do not understand is that the longer breath they have, the easier it is to sing greater. This doesn't appear correct for many, but is quite correct.

• Mother mother mom mom mom

The Mother exercise is a wonderful way to receive your voice reaching these high notes. Speak, don't sing the word mother on a scale. Thus, say mother about a five-tone scale or some other scale which you might consider. This assists in maintaining that larynx of yours impartial. The truth is that if ever your larynx, or your Adam's apple, extends up as you're singing, you're essentially damaging your vocal chords. Anxiety and anxiety will sense, but simply by performing the Mother exercise, it retains it steady and low.

Even if you sing higher from the Mother, it is going to help you regulate without attracting your larynx up significant.

Singing high notes might be hard sometimes, and learning how to sing high notes is certainly going to take a while. But simply by implementing the exercises and techniques above, you will be on your way to singing those high notes like a specialist.

Chapter 8

Doing it For a Living

Psalm 104:33
I will sing to the LORD as long as I live; I will sing praise to my God while I have my being.

Lots of men and women spend their lives dreaming of singing for a living, just to be disappointed since they never really learned how to be a singer. If you're among those men and women who likes to sing but you believe there is not expectation of realizing your dreams, now is the time for a reality test. Becoming a singer is not the tricky part, if you're enthusiastic about music. The trick to living a life filled with tune would be to establish realistic goals that enable you to earn singing your lifetime. It's still possible to wish for stardom however, even without popularity, your true fire could become your career rather than sitting behind a desk, expecting to be uncovered.

These suggestions below will instruct You How You Can become a singer for lifetime:
Before you can discover how to be a singer, then you must choose which sort of singing that you wish to do. There are several distinct forms of listeners, varying in design and favored audio kind.

Decide if you're thinking about pursuing solo work or if you would feel much better within a group, including a group, choir or quartet. You likely have some idea already of that course you want to mind, but create a well-defined selection and devote to it, hence the steps to attaining your objectives are succinct and clear.

Becoming a singer necessitates setting sensible targets. The likelihood of making it at the audio business, or being found and getting a fortune, are slim. Just be sure your real aim is to understand how to be a singer, not the best way to become wealthy and famous.

No matter how great of a singer you're, you need appropriate vocal coaching to become even better. If you have never had a vocal coach and sing just like a professional, your miles ahead of this match. But do not think you cannot improve even more. To understand how to be a singer, you must make your own, unique voice rather than copying another celebrity's style.

Additionally, you must have the ability to take and learn from comments, so constantly ask family members and friends for honest critiques. If a vocal trainer is too pricey, there are many sites out there to assist, such as ones who may teach you how you can sing online.

That is where many actors neglect or give up. Regardless of how gifted a singer you're, nobody will understand it unless you're out there promoting yourself. Apart from spending some time on procuring paying gigs via a promo kit, then you also need to visit music sites and promote your songs there and create connections, sing in local events at no cost, enter competitions, obtain expert letterhead and flyers, and advertisements your title wherever you may. You ought to be regarded as noticed.

But to be taken seriously from the music business or big music venues, you'll require a professional presentation and, ideally, a supervisor and representative to urge for you. These items all require a considerable quantity of effort and money. The most effective way to take would be to understand how to be a singer first, wait till there's a comfortable amount of fiscal stability and consistency on your music career, then go right ahead and reach for the stars.

CHECK OUT ELIZABETH'S OTHER BOOKS

(Her writings touch on over 50 different subjects.)

Encouragements For the Body Of Christ 3 Volume Set

Get The Whole Singbird Lessons Set Today!

Scripture Reference Guides

CHECK OUT BRIAN'S OTHER BOOKS

(his writings touch on over 400 different subjects.)

Call to Worship

Accept Jesus Today, there is No Other Way!

Our Call to Worship is from John 13:34-35, the words of Jesus:
"I give you a new commandment, that you love one another.
Just as I have loved you, you also should love one another.
By this everyone will know that you are my disciples,
if you have love for one another."
Let's pray:
Loving God,
we come to worship today because we love you,
and we want to love you more.
We come to worship needing love in our lives:
love for family, friends, strangers, enemies.
In this hour of worship,
touch our hearts,
fill our hearts,
open our hearts
to your love which passes all understanding. Amen.

Works Cited

Berchie, Daniel. *Bible*. Cambridge Scholars Publishing, 2016.

Copeland, Kenneth. *Our Covenant with God*. Harrison House, 1999.

Copeland, Kenneth, and Gloria Copeland. *From Faith to Faith: Devotional : a Daily Guide to Victory*. Harrison House, 1999.

---. *Pursuit of His Presence: Daily Devotions to Strengthen Your Walk with God*. Kenneth Copeland Publications, 2012.

"Course Textbooks | W. W. Norton & Company." *Home | W. W. Norton & Company*, books.wwnorton.com/books/college-subject.aspx?id=4294983309.

The King James Study Bible: King James Version. Thomas Nelson Publishers, 2008.

Washington, Booker T, and William L. Andrews. *Up from Slavery: Authoritative Text, Contexts, and Composition History, Criticism*. Norton, 1996.

Winston, Bill. *Faith & the Marketplace*. 2016.

---. *The Kingdom of God in You: Discover the Greatness of God's Power Within*. Harrison House, 2010.

---. *The Law of Confession: Revolutionize Your Life and Rewrite Your Future with the Power of Words*. Harrison House, 2009.

---. *Training for Reigning: Releasing the Power of Your Potential*. HigherLife Development Services, 2011.

---. *Transform Your Thinking, Transform Your Life: Radically Change Your Thoughts, Your World, and Your Destiny*. Harrison House, 2008.

World's Concordance to the Holy Bible: King James Version. World Pub. Co, 1969.

Hayward House

Publishing

hope.com:1532074000.jpg

hope.com:1532074000.jpg

hope.com:1532074001.jpg

hope.com:1532074006.jpg

hope.com:1532074706.jpg

hope.com:1532074715.jpg

hope.com:1532078735.jpg

hope.com:1532078255.jpg

hope.com:1532074037.jpg

hope.com:1532074356.jpg

hope.com:1532074735.jpg

Hayward's
Toy Television

1_rev copy
copy.jpg

1Untitled.jpg

3.jpg

4 copy copy.jpg

5 copy.JPG

6 copy copy.JPG

7 copy copy.jpg

8.jpg

9.jpg

9.jpg

10 copy copy.jpg

11 copy copy.JPG

12 copy copy.JPG

13.jpg

14.jpg

15 copy copy.jpg

16 copy copy.jpg

17 copy copy.jpg

18.jpg

19.jpg

20 copy copy.jpg

21 copy copy.jpg

22.jpg

23 copy copy.jpg

Get The Whole Series

Hayward House
Publishing

22559361R00025

Printed in Poland
by Amazon Fulfillment
Poland Sp. z o.o., Wrocław